What The Dogs Tell Me

I0116256

Rose Lesniak

RLDT🐾PRESS

For information address RLDT Press
645 NE 62 Street, Miami FL 33138

Manufactured in the United States of America, 2023

ISBN 979-8-9874185-0-5
Medium and Format: Print Paperback

Lesniak, Rose
What The Dogs Tell Me / Rose Lesniak
Synopsis: **What The Dogs Tell Me** opens a new chapter in
human-dog relationships.

Foreword

It was like she dropped down out of the sky, Rose Lesniak. Into the New York poetry world of the 70's and 80's with edgy feminist lines, her skate boarder joy and remarkable melting poet American blonde good looks Rose made a loud articulate splash for more than a decade and then she was gone. Poets die young, poets go off into the wilderness never to be seen again – there are so many ways poets vanish or quit, probably just as many myths as there are about dog's lives but never does a poet (or a dog!) go off and rescue kids in Florida from the carceral system (and their families!) then quitting that to train dogs. And not just train dogs, but know them, see them learn from them. One poem here is just a list of dog commands, the poetry we speak to them. Say it to yourself. Do it. Cause it's a gem and a gym. This is a how-to book in other words.

It's a poetry school and it's a dog school. If a writer is lucky their work gets translated into other languages, but Rose's one single language here represents our contract with animals mainly dogs on earth. This is a great volume of poetry, a radical one cause it's not human-centered and if you are a dog person – I've already spoken to the poets and reminded them of who Rose is and was – and what this is - but for dog people you have a treat in store for you, one you can chew on for a while or just treat yourself to occasionally when you've been good. What does this book do? Everything. In the energetic and ambitious manner of the Rose I know. But most of all it welcomes you and tells you how to read this book:

fall into the grass
And roll with this

and towards the end, she tells you that again. Because this is how you teach someone and that's how songs go too. They return.

She loves dogs because they are troublemakers. First you meet them where they are and make them comfortable and then they bark like hell. It's what we love about them. And Rose knows how to mourn dogs. There was Martha Washington, there was Martha Stewart and finally, there was her dog Martha who's gone. Alongside mourning the dog she's mourning her mother. An unending process. And it's just like losing your mother (I have, you will) to see how many words rhyme with mom and you just keep using those words like the mysterious holes the woman who birthed you has fallen in. Mom's gone and so is Martha. It's such a wise book. Sometimes (and these are my favorite poems) she the poet, the poem, the moment – with dogs is simply deeply present:

KNOCK KNOCK

I live
in a beautiful garden
I work in beautiful homes
I co-exist with beautiful minds
This excites me
Hello I live here
What is your name?

The poem ends with what you say at the beginning of any encounter. The encounter with a new dog is an encounter with life. And as a dog trainer she is encountering new life all the time. She is in the woods and she is meeting the people who live there. The more I revisit it I think this is the perfect job for a poet. And a dog lover. To go to work and love every day. Because dogs were sent to help us, and we are rejecting the message. There's a post-apocalyptic vibe, the apocalypse being the pandemic and everything else that is threatening our health and the health of the planet in our time. Dogs were "sent" to aid us in our struggles and our discoveries and if we reject their knowledge well it's simply biblical isn't it.

If in the end
Animals revolt
I will gloat.

Not until this moment did I realize what an animal word 'gloat' is – puffed up and shining and sort of throaty. She becomes an animal too in their triumph and their losses.

Because of that capacity (well all of them) she's more than a bit of a prophet. She's entirely comfortable with telling us what's wrong. It's the same old Rose, the ardent young feminist from the 70's who in the 21st C. still wants your ear:

THIS IS THE PROBLEM

Men can't have a child inside them
fix this and you can fix the world

But here she's almost looking at men like a dog. Is she man's best friend. What is it to be human, or not. When a cat is killed in the street she goes out and pushes it with her nose and goes "meow wake up". We all feel that way when someone is dead. That's what dogs do. And that's what the best poems do here in this book. Like one of my favorite poets, the 12th century Turkish poet Rumi, she doesn't so much end her poems as push you a little bit. She prods. Not like when you saw the dead cat in the street but when you saw what was great in the middle of your life, and you said hello to it because it knows you. And dogs are in the world with us so we can know we are here. They are our teachers and they protect us too. While we think we are owning them.

It's the other way around. Like everything. Read these poems. Rose knows. While she's training your dog, she'll train you.

Eileen Myles
Paris, September, 2022

What Readers Say...

After reading **What The Dogs Tell Me**, I need to "unstuck" myself and start reading poetry. I do believe you when you say "Dying doesn't bother me. Not being able to live does." Your book is definitely going to be around my house for all to read.

Dr. Catherine Kirchner, MD

What The Dogs Tell Me pays tribute to playful creatures who romp around without leashes, keep the secrets or smells, who sleep peacefully with no cares and can be silly & profound at the same moment. French president Charles de Gaulle wrote: "The better I get to know men, the more I find myself loving dogs." Lesniak's book reinforces that every day.

Lee Schrager
Founder South Beach Wine & Food Festival

Rose Lesniak's mindful listening gives spunky poetic voice; not only speaking for dogs, but as if dogs themselves were speaking to us. Her way of looking transports the reader to view as they see. There is a tender balance in these pages, of dealing with life's human trials and a desire to create a kinder world for canines.

Maureen Owen
American Poet

I anticipated a sensitive dog-oriented book of verses, and instead found a window into a deeper universe. **What The Dogs Tell Me** opened a portal to a bare, brave and honest soul.

Larry Bernstein, VMD. CVH. CVA. FAAD. PCHom

Tender inter-species poems from a dog's best friend. Sleeping with my dogs in bed. So what is family?

Anne Waldman
Author, "Fast Speaking Woman,"
"Trickster Feminism"

In an age of constant noise pollution, Rose's **What The Dogs Tell Me** is as clear as a dog whistle, calling you to come, listen and pay attention to what is around and inside you. It brings up memories, shares a mood, and opens you to connecting with dogs in a whole new way.

It's a must-read, an amazing opportunity to connect deeper with the world, people and the dogs around you.

Alexandra Rosen
Venture Forward Senior Director of GoDaddy

In the world of Marley, Lassie, Toto and yes, even Cujo, **What The Dogs Tell Me** is a true dog-listener story.

Tone Blevins
American Writer

Acknowledgments

For Chris, Tone, and Linda for your forever
guidance and support of my life and this book.

For the "Poker Girls" who will always carry
a card in my heart.

For all of my 7 angels who protect me from harm.

For Lisa who saved my life.

For all the Dogs and Parents who bring
me my greatest joy and knowledge.

And of course, my brother Joe.

Table of Contents

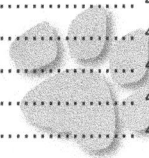

At The End of Morningside Park

Beauty is my own garden

Where new colors emerge.

The Brazilian orchids are flamed

As always this spring, my moments of joy.

Today Martha told me

That this is my meadow,

At the edge of Morningside Park.

My dogs know me, and I know them.

Fall into the grass

And roll with this.

Little Dog

Little silent dog

You are of great worry to me.

Who found you in the urban traffic?

You were happy you finally found me.

I will comfort and care for you.

I will kiss your nose so sweet!

Don't be afraid...

Look at me...

Here is a cooked piece of meat...

Sleep in my safe house...

Come on out for a walk...

Feel the sunshine on your back.

Pull up your head to smell...

Stand in the window for all to see you!

The amazing little dog is now free

And I am so proud, little dog,

To take your paw...

We look out at the

Beautiful world...

And bark like hell.

Dogs Out

The Cold

WINDS

Are coming in.

The Dogs

OUT

Dog Trainers' Lament

I used to say heel. Now I say smell it & let's go.

I used to be command respond. Now communicate & cue.

Everyone wants to communicate with who they live with.

It's so sad to see your spirit so sad

And we break it.

I used to say sit reward. Now I reward.

I used to say come over here right now!

And now I wait.

I used to be forceful & now I create.

I used to be scared walking past fast-moving objects

And now I'm not.

Slowly we come to another dog's face.

In the Morning

I see them walking

The dogs and their parents

                    I see them walking

And their pulling and pushing pulling and pushing.

Like...I don't know you

Like...I don't know what to do...

They say hello and really mean it

Means something

Vibrations mean more

Than intelligence...at this time

                    Young pups are coming

                    And I see them walking

In the cool times of Florida nights,

I see them walking

And I see them happy

Martha

She sat there in the corner like Martha Washington
she reminded me of her and her hair and it was the
day that Martha Stewart was indicted Martha was
meant to be with me and there she was there for my
whole life she taught me I needed to get out of my
situation in order to do something that I loved and
she's my girl and she stood by me for every important
moment in my life that I needed to do she was there
and suddenly she became older than me and I
switched and took care of her and I will be in her arms
when she leaves me for our next life when she will be
my wife.

Our Next Flight

Goodbye my baby girl

I will see you in our next life

We really had the greatest relationship, didn't we?

Today so peacefully in my arms you
moved to a higher plane

You will be sorely missed.

Martha peacefully put on her wings today at three

Off for a new adventure

Waiting for me.

In my next life.

Our next flight.

It's Been 10 Days
(For Martha)

The calendar is still on in September.

As if time stopped when you left me

In the car, driving

That song comes on

Reminding me of you.

It's been 10 days and still no sign

Please Martha give me a sign that you're ok.

Turning into Chase Bank

A woman is walking with her happy Wheaton puppy.

"You have a Wheaton baby!" I say to her.

"Yes!" she says

And "I love her!"

Then a rainbow appears.

Ok, Got it.

I'll move on.

To Dogs

Sometimes

        I wake up   middle of the night

Everything

            is too   LOUD

And I think of

             my childhood

The Shipwreck

            That story in my own hands

It gave me   FOCUS

Agree to pay millions to dogs

Loser

I don't care what your wealth brought you

If you can't make your dog happy

You're a loser

Baby.

Why Do Dogs Listen?

Fun things happen

When I'm around.

Martha Speaks
(For Tone)

Martha always told me what to do she tells me every night when we go to bed she tells me every night get up and go to the bathroom she told me you got to quit Child Welfare because it's going to kill you and do something that makes you happy I did that and I listened to Martha and I was at the computer in Surfside and she sat next to me and said pay that bill study the dog blessed ever since.

Counterconditioning

If you can't fix yourself

You will never fix the dog.

The Dogs 'n' Me

Ending dream

that moment

Your death

Your body

still holding.

In the San Francisco water

Hiding near a tree root

Lone ship to your right

Herstory of mass graves-

Swelling in the dusk sky

Seeking distance from hot and humid

My dogs laying with me.

Darkness Held My Soul

Darkness held my soul for a very long time

Tell me it's for real

I've seen it down in that box.

I like hearing sirens

They bring me comfort and

Ready to go

Deep into my bones let it go

And the dog lovin' group

Is happy

Sleeping with my dogs in bed

So what is family?

Rescue People

The sadness of eyes

As people fly by...and bye.

I don't know why I'm here.

I used to have a family...They loved me

And then went off to school

And walks stopped. Talks stopped playing stopped.

And I cried and acted out.

And they said I was not welcome.

Please take me home! I'm in a cage!

Rescue people I salute you

And how you do

The work you

Go thru...I salute you.

Stuck

So get yourself

Fuckin'

Unstuck

She's a Fuck

Planets drift by

I say hi

As dogs relax

I face the fact:

16 sessions too much

No breakfast no lunch

Get her to see

Her dogs tell her

What to be

When to be

How to be

All the same

As jumping up

She's in a funk.

Knock Knock

I live

In a beautiful garden

I work in beautiful homes

I co-exist with beautiful minds

This excites me.

Hello I live here

What is your name?

Apocalypse

When I chant

"Come on rain!"

The rain comes...

When I chant "Come here, boy!"

He'll be here

Tonight

To tell me who lives and dies.

Pandemic

In this version of our world

No one dares

To go underneath a monument.

A threat next door

A telescope sits.

Inside all of us...a new constellation.

5-G convergence of an August full moon

Brings heavy rains...Oh Miami!

Call overgrown ants

For help.

Above me, singing alone.

Chants as spells to soften

Purple iris in a golden vase

Over my dead mother.

Peace wraps itself over Chicago.

Where I climb back into my old ways of freedom.

You

You do not have to be

A Lesbian

To love me

Just love me

Corona Virus

Fix your inside

Not the outside

Covid Variations

Big sky

Fly

Don't die.

The Big Die

Sly

What a lie.

A Big Cry

Germs Fly

Not into I.

Germs fly

Into my eye.

I cry

I die

They lie

Don't fly

If you die.

The pie

In the Sky

Is wide open.

If in the end

Animals revolt

I will gloat.

Walking a Dog

NO ONE

Wants to be behind someone

Fumbling.

Force Training

Catholic school.

She pulled the back of my hair neck down

And forced the soap

Into my mouth.

Nun.

Done.

Success

Never killed me.

Fame.

Wood.

You Brought Me Out

(For Paula)

You don't have to connect with me

If you don't want to.

You'll be my wife

In my next life

Fresh

Smoky treats

Circe Circles

I turned them into animals

Because I finally had the chance.

And we were all happy and drunk.

You disgusting pigs.

                        And they all come back again
The dogs and men

                           They all came back

And we go on.

And I change you to a dog

To understand you.

I'm such a fool for you

And we love each other then.

                        You needed to learn a lesson.

               We're not your fucking slaves.

The next century we came to be brave.

And now You are the slaves

Slowly it will end

This way.

Pace

Just remember that the pace at which I proceed thru any training or behavioral modification protocol must be dictated by the dog's response.

I might sail thru one session or take weeks to achieve a certain response.

Be patient.

The most common mistake is moving too fast. Watch the dog, make sure she's relaxed. If not, go back to where she was comfortable...even if it's inside the house.

Then add distraction.

Then...more and more distractions. Reward.

Move to new heights.

Reward. And

Reward again.

COVID

I will not be afraid of Nature.

Nature is my friend.

And because I always thought of Nature

Nature will think of me.

Spare me.

I'm not afraid.

Of your viruses and dares.

Say+Say

I never wished I had a child.

I never regretted anything they say
                    I should be guilty about.

I'm learning. Isn't that what I'm supposed to do?

I've always taken risks

I've always kissed any lips I've wanted to...

I've never been good at long-term relationships.

My weak knee throws out my hip.

I have 96 years to figure it out

I gain wisdom from those I meet and am about

The life I geek.

We will rise and take over the planet...
                    I thought I'd return your coat

Thought you might be cold.

Today I lived 60 years 5 months 21 days 5 hours
+ 3 seconds.

Texas you just want to

Strawberry-and-whipcream it.

The river to me

Means homeland.

Everything causing serious problems

Will not go away

But me...

I see this and think. Can't help right now.

Reporters they say and say...

Never surprised me.

Feeding hungry people...

Understand the love part

They do not. I do.

And here I help with my dogs right now

I think they know they are helping too...

Miami summers are like a flu.

Staying around you...

You agree with me too?

We have to get rid of

The zoos.

Out There Somewhere

In the dark.

We urban girls

Yes, fear the night.

Can't walk a dog

It's late at night.

It just occurred to me

That indigos have taken form.

Lots of dogs

And now we walk.

And fuck you

Where have you been all my life?

Always wanted a family but never a wife.

This Banyan Tree
(For Barbara Barg)

Receives the migrating birds. And says I welcome you.

The pope says this too...

           The saved palm protects my song

           Because I brought her back to life.

I am working to see that dogs

Become companions to humans

Rather than slaves or computers

           Listen...

           The moon all red...

           Says thank you.

As we stop on the bridge normally shallow

Now a lake

In parking lots and doorways...

In cars or afar

Thank you for loving me inside this Banyan tree.

Positive, Positive, Positive

I want a dog not a robot the negative sides of positive based training. Sure I'm a positive-based trainer but what exactly does that mean? In my 20 years of training what I found was that positive based training means a lot more than just giving treats to dogs positive based training is all about being a positive based trainer because I know a lot of positive based trainers who are the most negative people in the world I want to be able to go into peoples' homes from house to house and be part of positive energy between animals and parents and myself. Just like there are all different types of people there are all different types of dogs I find that most positive-based trainers are constantly treating treating treating dogs. When really what they need is to look.

Positive, positive, positive.

Private Insanity

There is a place like Germany

In all of us.

And it wants to remain

A secret.

Textbooks were against us

From the very start.

Can't seem to remember

The words that knocked me

Out.

Belief System

I believe if one shuts the fuck up

Changes a dog's diet

Practices looking into their eyes

Practices calm walking

And teaches force-free

Dog basic commands

One can totally transform their relationship with their dog

Pandemic

I have nothing to do tomorrow.

And I exhausted my to-do list

What joy I have

To do anything I want.

Training 101

Keep going

to keep writing

to be your best

to keep helping

Take risks

Do what you love

Train to become

I like people and I like dogs

Spend the rest of your lives

Together...

We know who we are.

We remember each other

And the dogs come over to touch

And bother.

Joe

Joe was never really happy I picked him out of the group knowing he was from a puppy mill and decided this was my boy I already had Martha was such a great teacher and very stable so I took him in He bit 8 people by the time he was 2 years old He was scared and did not trust a dog paw or human hand a lot of this behavior was a reflection on how I was feeling breaking up with Candy so I got help chiropractor and mental health care Swimming and tai chi I had to deal with the environment he and I were living in a divorce that took 2 years to transform A lot of yelling and anger and I worked constantly on call and 10 hour shifts dealing with people who hurt children trying to figure out how I could help myself and make their lives better When I got home my partner was not there but you were So then I worked on you Counterconditioning to touch Teaching 2 steps back and look at me reward Calm walking twice a day getting him out from under the bath bowl He became stable as I became stronger And when he moved out with me we became together stronger

This is why God

Sent me the dog.

Habeas Corpus

I sign to you: I am crying. I try to talk to you. I love trees.

Why am I put in a cage?

I am crying. Crying. I want to be with you. Not able to move. Move in this cage.

I want to be a legal person!

Beg. Heel. Dance. Give me a chance to make my own choices. I am crying. Give me a chance. To have my own voice. I am crying. Crying. Punching myself in the face. Just sitting here. In my biomedical testing lab. Crying.

I used to be loved. He used to love the way I did that.

He used to love when I slept with him. I am crying. Crying. All by myself.

Held for research. It's an experiment. I am crying. Crying.

Finally held in your arms. We saved each other again.

Now we are going places.

Barking

Wherever you find a dog that is barking or upset you will find a lack of experience dealing with that.

Vision

Smell

Even if it's a big estate.

They're still in a cage.

You Love Me. I'm Scared.

Cool sheets of darkness

Cold water swimming in what you are...
        wow so different from I

That's your dog Joey

And he wants your attention.

The rain is pouring hard.

Like the love you have for me.

Bruised, unbalanced head I have...

We will never fight,

Because I will never give you the chance

To be that close to me.

Even if you feel the absence of...Never be sorry.

You are still my beautiful magnolia tree.

And I sit next to you

And everything smells so pretty. I finally have a mother.

Remember I have joy

Seeing Joey in your eyes.

People and Dogs

Too many poisons.

Too little

Real food.

Sierra
(For Chris)

This is

for you

my love.

You know

Who you are.

Art now is a Star.

Planet Poison

Acid

Water

Food

The acid is money

And this is what

Over and over

Our poor dogs are coming to.

People think if I smoke

I'm adding to the poison of earth.

But it really goes into me.

        We have our poisons

           Choose your poisons.

We are going to breathe...ready?

Don't lose your center.

I don't know why anyone would have a child at this time.

Ultra music...ringing in my ears.

Phrases My Dogs Know

Good morning. It's a beautiful day.

No agua!

Wait for Martha...

Let's go to the park.

What is that...?

Cross. Leave it.

Turn.

Stay.

Up...Look at me.

You have to wait...

Ok...out

Leave it!

Who wants to help mommy with the laundry?

Let's go for a ride.

The kitties have no mama. Leave them.

Hold on...Back.

I'll be right back.

Are you ready? Let's go for a walk...

Who loves you baby?

Go in the car.

WAIT. Let's go.

That's our friend. Go get em...

Mommy will be right back.

Under. Down. Jump.

Come over here.

Drop it.

Stay.

Who is that?

Time to eat?

Do you want to go to the park?

Martha, let me rub you...

Let me brush you...

Time to go to bed.

Good morning it's a beautiful day,

Stay.

For the Love of An Old Dog

How do I come here to be

laying next to you in the night

where the stars show us our

love outside the leaves falling

in darkness and the rain the

cool rain and the blasts of wind

on the holy roof

I am amazed that I love you

still so close to death and

much more than any human

on the corner of the bed

we breathe heavy into the air.

Joey

Where in my Joe?

That's what I want

To know.

Dying

Doesn't bother me

Not being able to live

Does

The New Cat

I'm sorry you lived a short life

Someone killed you with a car tonight

When I touched you, you were dead.

Your mom was there

Meow wake up

My love so short...my love so short.

Joe 2.0

Even as an Old Dog

His

Joy

Was the smell, my

Joe

Pretty Yellow Dog

Pretty yellow dog why do you draw your body away from me when my hand comes near your pretty yellow face dog why when I reach to you to try to say hi you pull away so far was it that first trainer who put his big hands around your yellow snout you couldn't breathe when he said you did it wrong and made you scared of hands this way was it the first trainer who hit you with a slap every time you wouldn't go into a sit I am sorry for that and promise that will not happen with me or what I teach the people you love I promise...

Yellow dog

Bigly's Welcome Treats

Welcome to our world. You have permission to enter
Bulldozed. Buried in trenches. Welcome come to our,
covered in sand, beneath the heels, decayed pine
world.

Hello old oak!
Smothered in bile
Toxined to death...permission to enter?

Welcome to our country of debris and
Carcasses of animals... Garbage in the streets.
Deformed legs, deformed lungs

Wings of tumors Trails of sadness...Cataracts in cars.

Dogs are welcome!
With permission we decline.
The blind and defective are in heaven.

Welcome to the rhetoric...Welcome to this place...
To bricks breaking Look up. Never had to before 9/11.
To the overgrown weeds and trash in the streets

Back to the grasslands.

Hello Wolfpack. I'm fuckin' strong.

The Truth
(For Jim)

The truth

Is not

Part

Of their

Program.

Sad Dog

When life is grey

And so are you

Let us think of something to do.

To bend your mind

To connect with mine.

Sad dog

Will not be blue.

Kibble

The dog food industry was created from human waste

Seemed appropriate in the 50's

Scientists were brought in to formulate this mush

Force the dog to like this delicious meal.

REALLY?

This is for You Joe

Certain places make me cry

And I give out a huge aaaaaahhhhh!

Today is such a day.

The sail opens

And the world is free to me.

As you watch from the air where you float...

You're still too heavy to leave our last goodbye

You're stuck there

Like me, Joe.

I love you boy.

As I hold you in my arms

And let you go.

Swimdog

I

Like   swimming with   you

We are moving

            and not talking

And we are   talking

As we swim

My Feelings Are This

If you have a good immune system

Nothing can kill you

That's the way bodies were set up

Get on with the world.

Pups have 16 weeks...

Fuck it up. Fuck the pup.

This is the Problem

Men can't have a child inside them.

Fix this and you can fix the world.

Why Dogs in America

You are my stuffed animal

I squeeze you and I love you.

Happiness means

He hit her in the head.

Dogs are sent here to get us

Off this planet...

Because...I thought I could save children and dogs

Made a wish-

Out of the darkness and into the sun

What have you both done today to make you feel proud?

When Men

Start wearing high heels...I will too.

The politics of sickness

Wrapped up for you.

Pity the Dog

Pity the dog

Dogs are protectors

Sent down to help us

Pity the dog

Sitting alone in a fog

Pity the dog.

Racing Extinction
(For Deb)

Water pumps

On Indian Creek Drive

There you are in the Northern Lights,

Trusted with all that money.

And I see my feet are dirty...I wash them

Killing the dirt never meant to live.

And the run

The run

The shelter dog loves.

I am the only one unattached to a computer tonight.

It happened...no oversight,

If the butterflies die...it's too late to fix them.

So damaged

It's not earth anymore.

Leak

Raining now.

Better not leak

As we sleep.

Moving for Marijuana

She moved out of state

Out of mind

Stop the seizures

State of Florida.

Ya Know It

Good work is when

Good work occurs   Ya know it...

When we are all one

And u get it and

We work and exchange

In the world we love   Ya know it

Now dying...

My darling loved ones

Flying in to help

Oh YYaasss   Ya know it

I don't think so.

Teaching a dog to connect   Ya know it

And we all win

In the end

The ones who get it

From Roof to Woof

I'm not interested in getting a dog to perform

Oh slaveowner

Oh mom

The hitting father...the City Council

I want to teach you

How to connect

So, you are happy

And so am I

Heal yourself

Put you in my body

Life is good

The circus of life

Jumping from roof to woof

Diamonds and Guns

Worlds always begin and end.

Ours is ending.

Dogs came to tell us

And help

They are too

Late.

The Dogs

The Dogs are leading us

To where we need to go.

Don't leave us

Alone.

I'm Heading (to Space!)

No I'm heading to space.

No

I'm heading to space. No I'm heading to space. No

I'm heading to space

No I'm heading to space

No, I'm heading to space

No

I'm heading to space.

No I'm heading to space

No I'm heading to space

No I am.

I'm heading to space...

The Cockroach

She keeps coming back.

I said I will not kill you

And picked up a paper and moved her outside

And she keeps coming back.

Today I found her drinking

Off a hot saucepan on the stove.

Savoring the remaining juice

From turkey I cooked for the dogs.

Howl

Exiled

from my own country

Exiled

from myself

Always a freak.

Until the week of   HOWL

I said, "Leave it."

And I did

And I left

Dog Slaves

In darkness

I awake at 6 AM to many dogs howling

A collective effort.

Dog Slaves.

We tell them what to do.

What to eat.

Force them to have shots

against their will.

Kill them when we want.

It's really an ugly existence

until the wise ones come forward

and mean business.

For Mom in the Bardo
(For Laurie Anderson)

You resemble the past

Gone dark where we lived

Gone dark

The yellow shelled kitchen table

Where we shared many tears

All vanished into emptiness.

For decades your families' wounds

Sucked you thru the keyhole

Into a future unprepared

Your standing there

My mother posing with her shotgun

By the door not letting me in

Mom It's me.

Now gone with the grief of her time.

This time

These times

Where she chooses to wander

Do not look back

Don't think of us here

Our light goes on

As long as we go on.

Mom.

She holds up in the Bardo

The great Chicago polka

Shuffling her dance.

So that she can

Dance again.

Looking For That Dog

Stay home.

No stress. Master class.

Think good thoughts.

Hang with a dog.

Talk to a dog.

No acid foods.

ProOmega Vitamin D B Boswellia complex

Vitamin C.

Immune boost 5 times a day

only water. Water in glass.

Cut down smoking.

Touch dog a lot.

Better to be hot than cold.

Spit it out.

A daily task no I will not wear a mask.

A little pot.

Remember chi grounding and practice positions.

Walk. Train outside.

Watch uplifting movies.

Talk to people you love.

Only eat what's growing

fresh in south Florida.

No sugar, no garbage,

no carbs,

no dairy,

nothing processed.

No anger at all.
Clean, clean, clean, throw away.

Imagine I'm fucking you.

Need to have more fun.

Starting tomorrow

looking for

That dog.

To Truly Know

Every time

I attend an appointment

workshop

conference

I learn something new.

To get me thru

BLOCK

And see the dog.

and see the human blooming...

I'm moving.

Why Are We So Fucked Up?
(For CK)

You let her out.

She goes in the yard.

Oh you have a big yard!

Oh so big.

¡Qué rico!

Dog goes out,

eats whatever shit he wants.

Dog barks when something new

comes close...

(Cause that's the

job I have...master.)

The cows and pigs are let out to graze.

They hit the ground and eat.

There's nothing much more to do.

Then we kill them.

And this is how we're raised and trained our loved ones?

To learn to graze...?

How wonderful our lives would be

venturing in the world

with

our best friend...our animal...

Not knowing exactly what's going to happen.

Next.

"But it is

so happening,"

She says to me.

(My job is now to be with you)

Before they kill us ...(with the edibles they've determined we can eat.)

Only...only...only...we eat...we eat we eat...chickens and cows....

We don't eat Dogs.

Because humans are hungry, they eat.

Oh, but not dogs. We don't eat dogs. We will eat pigs but not dogs.

We will eat bugs but not cows.

We eat beef but not chickens.

Really?

Walk with your cockroach

and teach it the fucking world.

And stop!

The fucking killing.

My Dogs Know Me and I Know Them

Beauty is my own garden

Where new colors emerge with the cold life

I lived with old loved ones.

The Brazilian orchids are flamed

as always this spring

For they are my moments of joy.

Today Martha told me That this is my meadow,

At the end of Morningside Park...

My dogs know me

and I know them...

Fall into the grass

And roll with this.

Drops of Martha's Medicinal Marijuana Oil

One for you.
One for me.

One for you.
Two for me.

One for you.
Three for me.

Me Too...Movement

Pete taught me the importance of driving a nice car.

Chass taught me... that what you believe was already created to believe.

Chucky showed me that sex could be fun.

Billy showed me good looking nice men can be evil.

Ulin taught me the body was one form and can become another.

Bob taught me that my opposite is the one for me.

Donald reminded me that creation of a child is the same as creation of anything.

Joey taught me to be strong...does not mean that you are The Strongest.

I can feel it...Master Rubio. Master Chen helped me see... Never move force with force.

Robin showed me you can die when you want to.

Todd taught me men can be very sexy just standing there.

Paul taught me how to scale a roof. Jump on trees.
Fight like a man.

Daniel told me your only loyalty is to yourself.

Fred showed me true intellect is a greater freedom
than obsession.

Carmen said, it's true art...if captured correctly.

Michael proved to me that marriage always turns to death.

Jerome taught me the finer manners
of living. Better to have the best.
Pay more for quality.
If someone cheats you...call him out right

Carmine showed me how to be a star.

Horrible experiences teach us.

How not to have horrible experiences.

When you've learned this much?

I think in percentages.

Insults To Dogs

Dead as a dog.

He left her like a dog.

He treated him like a dead dog in the street.

I wouldn't even do that to a dog.

Is he friendly?

He was an animal, he wasn't a human being!

It's like teaching an old dog new tricks.

I knew it was her time to die.

She treated me like a dog!

Before I met him he was a dog.

That dog don't hunt.

Beware of dog.

What dog doesn't bark?

He bit me like a dog!

You are like a dog with a fucking bone!

I can never let dead dogs lie.

I pee'd like a large dog.

If you lay down with dogs, you get up with fleas.

Even dogs have dreams

Not like machines.

More From Rose Lesniak

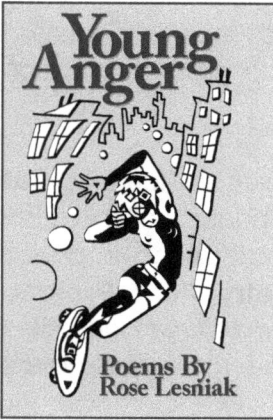

Young Anger

Like a young, vibrant, sugar high girl-woman, **Young Anger** skateboards into your brain and encourages you to Live, Do, Go, New York City. "Here it comes...ready?" You cannot sit still reading this debut poetry.

Circling around and screeching to a halt in the soul of a fresh young voice from the American heartland.

1st Edition published by **The Toothpaste Press**
ISBN 0-915124-34-3

Throwing Spitballs At The Nuns

A wonderful book-length poem about young memories and even younger ideas and ideals. Within a strict form, comes a radical voice for the voiceless, the restrained; 60's sentiment meets 80's energy. Listen well.

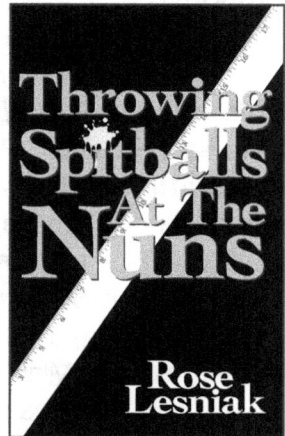

Listen Closely and hear the sound of social revolution!

1st Edition published by **The Toothpaste Press**
ISBN 0-915124-54-8

About The Author

Rose Lesniak was born and raised in Chicago. She graduated from Northeastern Illinois University with degrees in Education and Psychology.

In 1977, Rose moved to New York City, where she founded **Out There Productions.** This all-purpose poetic collaboration included magazines, poetry and videoperformances, poetry writing classes, and the **Manhattan Poetry Video Project**, the very first poetry/music videos. *Billboard Magazine* called this spoken word creation "a new short-form entertainment genre: poetry video."

They were a direct precursor to the fledging music videos of MTV. They premiered at the **Public Theater** hosted by Lou Reed. These performances introduced the wider world to established poetry legends like Allen Ginsberg, Anne Waldman, and Bob Holman. They also served as a teaching template for high schools and won a Blue Ribbon Award from the **American Film Festival.**

Rose's books of poetry include *Young Anger* and *Throwing Spitballs At The Nuns*. Her work can be found in *The Partisan Review*, *Poets' Encyclopedia*, *Poetry Project Newsletter*, and numerous small press magazines. She was featured on **Life is a Killer** by Giorno Poetry Systems. Her many on-stage performances at the **St. Marks Poetry Project** and numerous other venues were legendary.

Rose moved to Miami Beach, Florida where she worked as a Child Abuse Investigator with the Miami Beach Police Department until becoming a Certified Dog Trainer and Canine Consultant. Her latest book, *What The Dogs Tell Me*, is a direct reflection of her love for the canine world and the poetry universe.